Play Chess Not Checkers

The Practical Guide to Warm Start Your Dream Optometric Practice

Adam Ramsey, OD

© 2020 by Dr. Adam Ramsey.

All rights reserved. No part of this book may be reproduced, stored in a retrieval system or transmitted in any form or by any means without the prior written permission of the publishers, except by a reviewer who may quote brief passages in a review to be printed in a newspaper, magazine or journal.

First printing

Front Cover Photography by KVLmedia
https://www.kvlmedia.com

Front & Back Cover Design by iMedia Marketing Group, LLC
http://www.imediamarketinggrp.com

ISBN: 978-0-578-61720-6
PUBLISHED BY SOCIALITE VISION

**Printed in the United States of America
Play Chess Not Checkers...**

"Dr. Ramsey has done a great job at breaking down the dizzying process of starting an optometry practice. His insight has been invaluable to me and my practice and I'm excited that he is now in a position to share that insight with even more owners. This book is basically a step-by-a step guide to getting it done right the first time and opening warm, not cold."

Danielle Jackson, OD President of Jackson Eye

"Dr. Ramsey distills a complex process with tons of moving parts down into an accessible recipe that any of us can follow. I may not have taken the plunge yet, but this book demystifies the process and makes me feel like I can do it."

Andrew Brauer, OD

"Play Chess, Not Checkers lays out a blueprint for doctors like myself who are looking to start this journey of optometric entrepreneurship. Dr. Ramsey shares valuable pearls and provides insight, in a very understandable way, which helps breed confidence to anyone who has an urge to step out on their own. This book is a must-read if you truly want to establish success more sooner than later when starting a practice 'warm'."

Adam Young, OD

"Thanks for all the work that went into this. Wow! It will be a classic."

Terry Bonds, OD Owner of Lifetime Eye Health

DEDICATION

This book is dedicated to the mother that raised me Arlene Hagley. You created the entrepreneur you see before you and without you I'm not sure what I would have become. This book is also dedicated to my wife, Chrissi-Lee Ramsey, the queen of my household and the love of my life. You make life worth living. I have the energy to continue my passions from the strength and grace you show me every day.

TABLE OF CONTENTS

Introduction
Meet Dr. Adam Ramsey

The Amateur - Arrange Your Pieces
Make The Decision
Reasons Not To Open Warm
Begin With The End In Mind
Build Your Credit!
Get Experience In Private Practice
Begin Writing Your Business Plan
Build Your Savings
Get An NPI & CAQH Number
Incorporate & EIN
Trademarks And Copyrights
Open A Checking Account

Middle Game - Make Your Moves
Hire Consultant & Join Buying Group
Find A Potential Space
Research & Talk With Lenders
Design Your Space
Obtain Buildout Quotes
Branding
Online Presence
Begin Remodeling
Phones, Internet, And Alarm System
Insurance Credentialing
Now Hiring!
Choose An EHR
Frame Inventory
Equip Your Office

Office Supplies

End Game - Checkmate
Policies & Procedures Manual
Train Employees
Marketing Campaign
Open House
Open For Business!

The Master Checklist

Appendix

INTRODUCTION

"Avoid the crowd. Do your own thinking independently. Be the chess player, not the chess piece." - Ralph Charell

The purpose of this book is to prepare you to open the doors to a successfully independent optometry practice. Ask one hundred doctors exactly how they did it, and you'll receive one hundred different answers. I've condensed those unique experiences and my personal experience into this step-by-step guide - the premiere strategy towards the practice of your dreams!

Meet Dr. Adam Ramsey

I was born on the island of Trinidad and Tobago and grew up in Pembroke Pines, Florida. I attended The University of Florida and obtained a degree in Health Education graduating with honors. I also graduated from the Southern College of Optometry in Memphis in

2012. I always knew I wanted to be in private practice and working for myself. I didn't appreciate people telling me what to do so my WHY was simple - to be fiercely independent.

While in school, I was the Vice-President of NOSA, FOSA and attended every single private practice meeting we had. I ended up winning a scholarship to attend a Cleinman Performance Partners meeting, and sat in a room full of millionaire optometrists who shared their secrets on how to operate more effectively. I participated in a business plan writing contest with a good friend of mine, Dr. William Tantum. We placed second, but I believe we won, and the judges tallied the votes incorrectly.

During my fourth year of optometry school, I started looking for jobs and career options. On one of the placement sites where I posted my information, an optician reached out to me saying, "Hey I have an optical in Stuart, Florida and we're looking for a doctor to work independently next door." I wasn't looking to move to Stuart, but I flew down to explore the opportunity anyway. After checking the place out, I signed on with what I thought were great terms and was on my way to being a real independent doctor. Fast forward six months later, I moved to Stuart, bought fancy grown-up furniture, rented a cool townhouse and ordered all the equipment and supplies I needed.

A week before we were scheduled to open, the optician called and asked me to swing by. When I got there all I saw were boxes everywhere and frames coming off the wall. How naive of me, when I see the situation, to ask, "If we were painting why didn't you say so? I would have come prepared to work." He begins to tell me that he decided to close the store instead of trying to turn it around with the fresh energy I was bringing in. I had five minutes to pack up $10,000 worth of equipment into the back of my station wagon and drive off. As I was driving, I couldn't help but think about how I spent every dime I had and banked on seeing some patients next week to make my money back! I just went home, wiped away my tears and started looking for a job. I applied to everything available within an hour's radius of where I lived. While waiting for replies, I picked up fill-in work. Since I was in transition, I kept my white coat and supplies in the car and worked in four to six different offices per week for the next several months. It was a crash course in optometry and I learned more than you could imagine during that time period. I obtained an interview with American Optical Services, the top private equity group of 2012 (before My Eye Doctor and other private equity groups came into play). I walked out of that interview with an office of my own in West Palm Beach!

After nine months of the sweetest gig a guy could ask for, I got a call to go to a steak dinner with my manager, who lived in North Carolina and oversaw the office remotely, the following week. In my head, I'm thinking this is great! I wrote down a list of things I wanted to fix and what we needed to do to improve the office. I arrived at the restaurant, found a nice table and we placed our orders. My manager proceeds to tell me that although the practice increased by thirty percent since my arrival nine months ago, they are closing the store and selling all assets. I immediately lost my appetite. Once again I found myself as the traveling optometrist. It was at that moment I decided that I needed to work for myself and that I wouldn't let people or corporations control my destiny. I opened up Iconic Eye Care three months after that meeting.

Disclaimer: *I have created a list of action items that I consider most important when opening your dream optometric practice. I am not a legal expert. In this book you will find my strategies, opinions and personal experiences. Results may vary, please consult an attorney for the legal requirements regarding opening your new business.*

THE AMATEUR
Arrange Your Pieces

"It is not a move, even the best move, that you must seek, but a realizable plan."

- Znosko-Borovsky

What I've realized more than anything on my journey to business ownership is that the devil is in the details and preparation is key. The pep talk is over. The remainder of this book is your winning strategy. The following moves may be made somewhat out of order depending on your exact circumstances, but each step must be thought through.

In chess, the first ten to fifteen moves indicate the beginning, or opening of the game. It is characterized by the rapid development of forces and control of the board. Once the decision has been made to begin and after doing some thorough research, the first step to starting any business is the financial stuff. You need to get money from somewhere to start your business, and the government has to be able to track and tax it.

Make The Decision

In the introduction, I discussed my reasons for starting my private practice. Before you begin your journey, you will have to do the same. Ownership is a marathon, not a sprint, and without the right motivation, you won't be able to endure. Why do you want to own your own practice? Write this down. Remember, money can be motivating, but it may come much later than you expect it to. In the beginning, starting an optometry business may mean taking a pay cut or working overtime to match the wages you earned as an employee. It's normal for a new business owner to take about five years to match their previous income. Consider other motivational factors as well, such as professional autonomy, community involvement, and service opportunities.

Exercise: What is your WHY? Write your answer in the space provided.

_____

_____

_____

This book is about opening warm, but some of you may not know what that truly means. A cold start practice is one that is opened without any previous patients and starting from scratch. This book will teach you the strategies you'll need. When you open the doors to your brand-new practice, you'll actually have people that will want to use your services right from the beginning. With the right preparation, you can be years ahead of another business that did not have a plan of action. Failure to plan is planning to fail.

Reasons NOT to Open WARM

So you've written down your reason for owning a practice. Well, before you sign the lease to a grey shell of an office consider all the ways that you can become a business owner before a warm opening. If you have exhausted these strategies and still want to move forward, then you know you are truly ready. About eighteen months in, when you find yourself second-guessing every decision you've ever made in your life, you will sleep better knowing that this was your primary goal and better days are ahead. There are ways that you can own your own private practice, without having to start from scratch. Consider the following as alternatives to opening warm.

BATTERY

Lining up two pieces that move similarly, like a Queen and Rook or Queen and Bishop.

The first option I would explore is buying an existing practice. There will always be people willing to sell, but the question is should you buy? I would encourage you to buy an ugly busy practice, instead of a beautiful slow practice. You can make it pretty over time, but no matter what you do you cannot increase revenue in one weekend. The benefit of purchasing an existing practice is the existing staff who know how to effectively do their jobs. You do not have to know how to file claims from day one since Beth has been doing that for ten years. You will have a framework that you can adjust and make your own. Now, having existing staff is not always the best since they may push back on the new way of doing things and refuse to adapt to a new culture. You will also have patients that say *Dr. Smith never charged me for that* or *I cut his grass so I don't pay for anything when I come here.* There are pros and cons that come with this type of situation. You want to make the best move for you and your comfort level. Getting financing is easier with an established practice since the bank uses the P&L and tax returns from an existing business to justify the sale. In some cases, you can get the seller to finance a portion of the sale and that would give them more of an incentive to assist in the practice's success after the sale.

Now, remember I said to look for a busy practice. In evaluating existing practices, the profit made from the practice is how you will pay for the monthly loan payment. For example, if it takes between $150,000 – $250,000 to open and establish operations, then I would not pay $200,000 for a practice that only did $300,000 the previous year. I could accomplish that on my own with a brand-new business. But if the practice did $300,000 and they were selling it for $90,000 that would be something to consider. Or if they were doing $500,000 and wanted $175,000, then that might be a better deal since you are getting three years ahead in sales and have a decent starting point. I used gross numbers in the examples above, but I would prefer to compare practices based on the net income not gross.

Most owners do not discuss these figures when talking about their practice. I would much rather have a $500,000 practice that nets 40 percent than a million-dollar practice that nets only 20 percent. You can increase the gross easily when you have the correct systems in place, but fixing the net is the subject of another book. Any numbers I throw around are only examples and I implore you to consult with a professional accountant before making any purchases.

MATERIAL

A way to determine piece value; or the winning of a pawn (or piece, or Exchange) means winning "material".

The next option you should explore is joining another successful doctor in town. Join your local association if your city or county has one and attend meetings. If you go to enough meetings, then you may run into the doctor that has more patients than he or she can handle. On the other hand, you may find the doctor looking to slow down and wanting the new doctor to come in and allow them to use that new RV they just bought. If you're a specialist, then that's even better! You could market yourself and other doctors may come to you and ask if you would consider joining their practice.

Imagine a situation in which you say, "My name is Mary and I completed a residency in Low Vision at a private practice in DC. There I saw how we were able to increase profits by adding this service to the practice. I would love the opportunity to bring my knowledge and expertise to your practice." Doctors, whom you never expected to interact with, may reach out to you and offer you a position in their office. The only caveat with this option is if you want to be an owner at their practice, make those intentions clear from the start. Ask for a written contract outlining a path to ownership and an evaluation of the practice at its current value. Don't wait until after you've helped to double the value and have to pay a higher price.

PROMOTE

When a pawn reaches the other side of the board, the 8th rank, it can promote to a Queen, Rook, Bishop, or Knight on the promoting square.

Some doctors will tell you that after you gross or net a certain amount you are allowed to buy-in. They might specify a time period that needs to elapse in order to become a partner. The benefit of this strategy is that you do not take a hit in income that you would have received by opening cold. You would have an increase in income and be able to learn from another established doctor along the way. Don't get me wrong, this is not without its fair share of complications. As the associate doctor, you will have to earn the respect and loyalty of the established patients. You could ask yourself whether this will ever be your practice too or will you always be Dr. Smith's new associate. You will have limited decision-making and judgment calls on how the practice is run and what systems are in place. I say all that to say this, the most profitable optometrists across the U.S. are in multi-doctor practices. You get to see more patients, have less overhead and costs to operate the business, and maintain a steady rise in profit. This strategy puts you about five to ten years ahead if you can find the right situation to work out.

SKITTLES

Chess for fun or chess without a clock; a skittles room is where you go and play for fun while waiting for your next formal pairing.

The last option you'll want to consider is starting in a commercial setting and transferring to a private practice after three to five years. With this strategy in play, I want you to understand that not all situations are created equal. You will need to sign the lease in a way that ensures that you maintain ownership of patient charts, not the corporations and this will differ in the state in which you practice. Anywhere that has free eye exams will not allow you to maintain your own charts.

The upside to this option is that you learn half the business while building your brand in the community. You will learn how to sell eye contacts, dry eye products and learn proper billing protocol in this setting. You'll need to see patients at least two times for them to be more connected to you than with the office at which you work. This may take three to five years depending on how frequently patients in that area take care of their eyes. You have to go into this practice setting with the end goal in mind. If you don't plan to leave, then you never will.

You need to pay close attention to your lease and non-compete radius before signing the contract. There is a benefit to this practice model but at the end of the day, no matter what you do, it is not your business and they can ask you to leave at any time for any reason. Lots of doctors make a good living doing this, but you need to understand that you are putting your future and livelihood in the hands of a corporation. Ask the doctors at Sears or Shopko if they thought they would lose their business without much notice.

Make sure you own the website domain, phone number, credit card machine and electronic health records. If you pay the bill you can move it when you decide to leave. Patients are connected to a phone number and website, so if you have that, you can still be connected to your current patients after you move. I would encourage you to request updated email addresses from your patients since that would be the easiest and most cost-effective way to connect with them after your departure. After you have exhausted all of these options, if you still want to be in private practice, then continue reading this book about how to open warm and be successful.

Begin With The End In Mind

TEMPO

The "time" invested in developing the pieces harmoniously. A pawn is said to be worth three tempi, or three turns.

What's your end goal? What does a successful business look like to you, and what happens when you're finished with it?

_____

_____

_____

_____

There is no wrong answer to your ideal end, but whatever yours is will help you determine how, when and even where you may need to begin. It's never too late to make the decision about practice ownership, but the sooner you do the better. Preparations for entrepreneurship can begin as early as optometry school.

What would your perfect successful office look like?

_____

_____

_____

_____

I would suggest taking some time to be creative with this next step and realize the name of a business sets the tone and atmosphere for the business. You could use your last name or some variation of your name in the business name which makes the process much quicker. I want you to think about when you go to sell your hugely successful practice thirty years from now, how this could affect the next doctor who might want a practice name of their own. If you grow to add an associate, will patients want to see anyone not listed in the name of the practice?

What are you going to name your business?

_____

What words stick out when you think about your business?

_____

_____

You need to write out a vision and a mission statement. These will be the guiding principles in which all other decisions about the office should be based on. A Mission Statement defines the company's business, objectives, and approach to reach those goals. A Vision Statement describes the desired future position of the company. Elements of mission and vision statements are often combined to provide a statement of the company's purposes, goals and values.

Mission Statement

_____

_____

_____

_____

Vision Statement

_____

_____

_____

_____

You have selected a name and written out your mission and vision statements. Now you need to secure the website domain and social media handles for your business. I would suggest getting a few domains that are close to the business name you chose. Below is a quick list of suggested social media sites on which to secure your business name. These platforms do not need to be active immediately, but you want to ensure their availability before putting time and energy into a name that you do not have full control of.

Social media sites to consider:
- Google My Business
- Facebook
- Instagram
- YouTube

Build Up Your Credit!

Begin to work on your credit profile as early as possible. For most people, opening a practice means asking someone for a LOT of money. You can start by checking your credit score and credit reports. A good credit score is an indication to potential lenders that you can handle repayment of a loan. A website like Credit Karma can be helpful in tracking any changes to your credit; although the scores they show are not the exact scores a lender will use. You can get a free copy of your credit report from any of the three bureaus by visiting the website www.annualcreditreport.com.

SKEWER

Sometimes called an "x-ray" attack, a sort of inside-out pin. A move that attacks a piece of value, but there is a piece behind it of equal or lesser value that will be captured anyway if the attacked piece moves.

You will need at least a 640 credit score to be approved for a business loan, but you'll qualify for more money and lower interest rates if your scores are higher. Your debt-to-income ratio, payment history, and credit card usage are used to determine your creditworthiness. If you don't already have a credit card, get one. To avoid added interest fees, use your cards to purchase small things that you would be able to pay off completely each month. The caveat is you never want the balance of your cards to exceed 30 percent of your total credit limit. Large revolving balances can lower your credit score. If you have any loans, continue to make your payments on time. Getting sixty days or more behind can also put a huge dent in your scores. The debt-to-income ratio is usually the biggest problem for newly graduated medical professionals. We have big debt without much income to balance it out. The way around this is to ask for money sooner than later. The longer you're out of school the more money the banks will expect you to have. We will touch on this topic later.

My credit report showed me:
- Great - ready to move forward
- Borderline - I need to clean up a few things first

- Worse than I thought - time to regroup and come up with a new game plan

Gain Experience In Private Practice

Use your weekends to shadow or work for a doctor that has a practice you admire. Make mental notes of what you like and don't like about how the office operates. Get to know the lead optometrist and ask for behind the scene looks at the practice. Sit in with them while they do things outside of patient care - these are tasks we don't learn in school. Ask how they got started and what their growth was like in the early years. Sit in while they pay bills, file claims, and process payroll. How do they delegate all of the administrative tasks? This running list will help you to write your business plan, design your office and develop a sense of your office culture.

What are some of the things you loved about offices you have visited?

_____

_____

_____

_____

What are some of the things you disliked about offices you have seen?

_____

_____

_____

_____

What could have been done to improve those offices?

_____

_____

_____

_____

How do you want people to describe your practice?

_____

_____

How do you want your patients to feel when they step into your practice?

What do you want your practice to be known for in the community?

Begin Writing Your Business Plan

Writing a business plan can be a daunting task, but a good plan is necessary to get started. Downloading a business plan template will help to organize your thoughts, describe your ideal practice, estimate start-up costs, predict financial growth and prepare you for the loan application process. At this point, you may not have all the information you need to complete your business plan. Also, note that your business plan is a dynamic document meant to be adjusted and amended as the business grows.

TACTICS

The mechanics of combining piece moves and creating threats; involving piece safety, checks, attacks, etc. Advanced tactics are considered "combinations" of tactical motifs, such as pins, forks, removal of the guard and so forth.

Supply and demand is the most basic premise of economics. Sellers need buyers and vice versa. Before you invest time and money in starting your practice, make sure your services will be needed. Where do you want to practice? Do you prefer a specific neighborhood, city, state, region or climate? Are you open to whichever area might have the best opportunities? Write this down. Collect demographic information on possible locations. City-data.com is an excellent resource. How many eye care providers are currently in the area? Ten thousand people to one optometrist were the numbers I learned in school. I believe that, at the time of writing this book, if you could get closer to a ratio of five thousand to one that would be a safe place to start in a more urban setting. The next number I would look at is the number of dentists in the area. This number has stayed steady at three dentists to one optometrist in a city. The reason for this is that people get their teeth cleaned about three times more than they get their eyes checked. These statistics don't apply if you build a specialty practice. Having other offices nearby could actually work as referral sources in this case. For the rest of the book, I will only refer to primary eye care or family practice, but you can adjust the information to the specialty of your choosing.

What are the top three cities or towns you would like to open a practice in?

_____

_____

_____

Time To Build Up Your Savings

Many ODs think that private practice is the way to fortune and fame. It can definitely be a lucrative deal, but making the decision usually involves a pretty hefty pay cut for at least a couple of years. Before you begin looking for a bank to give you money, get your own financial house in order. Save as much money as you can since you will need to put some skin in the game through this process and having money available to you will always help along the way.

FORFEIT

When a player doesn't show up for a game he is forfeit and loses.

There will be months when you can't pay yourself from the business due to cash flow miscalculation or when you need to fund your practice from your personal account. I could give you an arbitrary number but every situation will be different. A goal of six months of expenses saved for yourself is a good starting point. Most banks will require you to work three days a week outside of the business to support yourself. Therefore, you need to be able to survive on three days a week income. So if you work 5-6 days now, save the income from those other 2-3 days. Put money aside for a year and then you will have a savings. Also, teach yourself to live on less since that is the road you are destined to embark upon.

Can you live on three-day week's salary?
- Yeah, sure I am frugal.
- No way! I might need to sell a kidney!

Get An NPI and CAQH Number

NPI stands for National Provider Identifier. It's a unique 10-digit number assigned by the Centers for Medicare and Medicaid Services (CMS) to health care providers in the United States. Commercial insurance companies use this number during administrative and financial transactions. For the fastest receipt of an NPI, use the web-based application process. Log on to the National Plan and Provider Enumeration System (NPPES) and apply online at https://nppes.cms.hhs.gov/#/. After successfully completing the application, you'll receive two NPI numbers. The first is your individual identifier and the second reflects your business. These numbers will stay with you as long as you remain in business. Use caution regarding the information you put in the application since this is considered public information. Patients, insurance agencies and government entities will have access to any phone numbers and addresses listed unless you use a post office or private mailbox.

Next, you will need a CAQH, or Council for Affordable Quality Healthcare number. This is an online database where insurance companies will verify your provider information. This needs to be updated on a quarterly basis. You can make your information available to as many or as few companies as you desire. Maintaining accurate and up-to-date information will make the credentialing process go much smoother.

Provider NPI: _____

Business NPI: _____

CAQH: _____

*Maintain these numbers for your own records.

Incorporate & EIN

The next step in starting a business is registering with your state. There will always be a debate on choosing an LLC or S-Corp. And the answer to the question is that it depends. I advise you to consult the CPA that will be doing your taxes and explain your financial situation and they will help you pick what is right for you. At the end of the day there is no wrong answer it's just the way you file your taxes but at the end most would say it works out about the same depending on who is doing your taxes. You can file the paperwork yourself by following the directions on your secretary of state website or pay a lawyer or online service to do it for you. This process will grant you an Employer Identification Number (EIN) also known as a Tax ID#. This is basically your business's social security number and you will use it regularly.

EIN: _____

Trademarks And Copyrights

I started this chapter by talking about purchasing your domains, creating social media handles, writing your vision and mission statement and having a plan for the type of business you want. The next topic is trademarking. Because there is so much to cover regarding this topic, I felt it needed a section of its own.

CAPTURE

(or Take) not Kill – to remove a piece from the board via a legal move.

The subject of trademarking is very personal and I wanted to take my time when discussing this section. To be honest, having issues with trademarks is what inspired me to start writing this book. Here's my trademarking story.

I incorporated Iconic Eye Care in May 2012. When I started my business, I read every optometry business book on the market twice and none of them educated me on how to properly trademark anything. What I did not know was that VSP had the first usage of Iconic in 2011, although they had not used the trademark or made it public until after I had already started my business in 2013. What I learned is that a trademark includes the way a word is pronounced and covers other languages. So after operating my business for SIX years, I was forced to change the name due to a trademark.

FORK

A double attack, usually by a Knight or Pawn (thus looking like a "fork" in the road), a common chess tactic.

My business is now known as Socialite Vision. At first, I was very upset and wanted to kick and scream. But after I got that out of my system, I realized that this is a business. I needed to take control of my name and brand. I was taught a major lesson and I hope by sharing my story no other business owner would have to go through what I have. Before you start on this entrepreneurial journey, research and apply for the trademark of your name.

What exactly is a trademark? A trademark, or trademark, is a word, phrase, symbol, and/or design that identifies and distinguishes the source of the goods of one party from those of others.

You can have the domain and even have your company listed on a state licensing board, but the national trademark is what matters when you broadcast your brand to the world. The eye care industry has lots of money and companies invested in seeing these brands grow and be sold. Most offices do not consider trademarking their practice names, so if you're going to do it then do it right and trademark your name. Now I will warn you the process is not easy or quick, but once you own your trademark it can never be taken away from you. You may have to be super creative to come up with something that will be accepted as a trademark, but when you succeed you will have protected your brand.

PIN

An attack (by a Rook, Bishop or Queen) on a piece that cannot or should not move, because a piece behind the attacked piece is worth even more. If the piece behind is a King, this is an "absolute" pin and the pinned piece is not allowed to move, or it would put the King into check.

Obtaining a trademark is only good if you are willing to defend it. Having a trademark does not stop another company from copying your name and opening up a similar business. What having a trademark does is allow you the protection from another business claiming that you are infringing on their trademark when you have the documentation to prove otherwise. Begin by searching existing trademarks with names in the private offices' category, which is Class 44. The United States Patent and Trademark Office's site is where this journey starts. You can visit it here - https://www.uspto.gov. If you don't see an exact duplicate, then it's time to hire a trademark attorney to perform a deeper and more comprehensive search. It can take up to a year to get a trademark issued so start this process early.

To trademark or not to trademark that is the question:
- I am the gambling type - let's roll the dice!
- I am not taking any chances – I'm going to choose a name I can trademark.

Open A Checking Account

You will need a business checking account before you can get a business loan. Getting connected to a bank that will offer you the services of a personal banker is the most ideal in my professional opinion. Bank of America and Wells Fargo are the two biggest banks that have programs that understand the needs of optometry practices. The primary issue I've seen with using big banks is that decisions are not usually handled locally. If you need extensions and exceptions, the loan officer you are working with cannot help and will require the approval of a manager or someone who is not in the same building. Credit unions and community banks will give you a more personalized experience during the loan application process. Developing relationships with smaller banks and local credit unions can go a long way in your career. When opening personal and business accounts, I would ask for a low-interest-rate line of credit. Banks are trying to earn your business so they are willing to work with you. Later in the book, we will go over getting a loan for your business.

MIDDLEGAME
Make Your Moves

"Life is like a game of chess, changing with each move."
Chinese Proverb

The middle game in chess follows the opening. The plans that were formed are put into action based on your current position.

Consider Hiring A Consultant And Joining A Buying Group

Consultants can help you envision the business you want. They will lead you down a path of questions and your responses to these questions can yield the practice of your dreams. You can do it without a consultant, but you may also waste money and start slower than you desire to. That is the trade-off for the cost of hiring a consultant. Most banks will not pay for soft assets such as a consultant, so expect the cost to come out of your working capital or other designated funds. Remember all that money I told you to save? Well, here is a spot you may have to use it for if you choose to hire a consultant.

Private practice optometry is a tough business and there are lots of ways to lose money, yet only a few ways to make it back. If you try to go at this by yourself, it will make this road a lot tougher. You are stronger together and as you start this journey you need a partner and guidance. You can seek the help of consultants like The Visionaries Group, The Williams

Group, Icare Advisors, Power Practice or Cleinman Performance Partners.

You will also need the help of buying groups like Vision Source, IDOC, PECAA, Vision Trends, Healthy Eyes Advantage or PERC. One of the benefits of joining a buying group is you get a discount on goods and services when your volume is too low to get those discounts on your own. These groups have pre-negotiated pricing on pretty much everything you'll need in an office. Now the way the group is structured and partners that they align with will be different. You can either pick your partner companies and then find groups that will give you the best discount, or pick the group and then use the partner companies they have aligned with to provide you the most value. Each of these groups has their own secret sauce to what it takes to create a successful private practice. Either one of these options can work for you if you know how to work them. Every doctor you talk to will have their own opinion about why you should use this one and not use another, but you'll need to do your own research and find the best fit for you.

Find A Potential Space

There are three things that are difficult to change when looking at a space: lot, layout and location. First things first, pick the right location for the specific type of practice you are looking to open. If you seek to provide vision therapy, then being in a plaza with a school and a pediatrician would be an excellent combination. If you want a high-end boutique, then go where the money is. You can change wall colors and flooring in a weekend, but you can't pick up and move if you open and realize you are in the wrong part of town for the type of practice you want. When comparing potential locations, finding one that requires the least amount of build-out cost to make it functional should be of the highest importance. If it is a grey shell and has never been built-out before, many landlords will assist in cost or give rent concessions to make the space usable.

After you have found the perfect spot on the best corner with lots of natural light, you'll need to eventually sign on the dotted line and secure your slice of heaven. I cannot stress enough the importance of seeking legal advice from an attorney that handles these negotiations regularly. You are in the position of power and everything is up for negotiation. In most cases, you can get free rent during the build-out phase too. The amount you must pay as a deposit on the space can change and get refunded IF you are a good tenant.

Deciding on how long of a lease you want will also be a sticking point. If you pick a small office, you may want a shorter lease thinking you will outgrow it sooner. If you pick a larger space that costs more to build out, you may want a longer lease to allow you to recoup that initial investment. I prefer the five-year term with an automatic option for another five without negotiation that gives you freedom and flexibility.

One of the most important lessons I learned after opening my practice was that 95 percent of my customers found me after receiving the address and phone number. Did I need class A real estate on the first floor with street frontage? Probably not. Those people would have found me on the second floor of a medical complex. With the right situation, I can see someone opening with a lower overhead cost to allow his or her money to stretch further. The benefit of the first floor is that elderly and disabled patients have greater access to you, someone can hop out of the car and grab contacts more easily, and in the era of Amazon convenience is still KING.

Time to design with your third eye:
- I am a creative person and want a grey shell location.
- I would like to find a location that requires the least amount of construction.

Research & Talk With Lenders

Time to address the elephant in the room - the money. As you consider opening a private practice, the most common hurdle you'll face is thinking about how you're going to afford everything. It's a legitimate concern and understanding cash flow is very crucial. As far as I know, Bank of America and Wells Fargo have had the best lending options and resources to open a medical practice. When comparing offers, you'll want to look at who will offer the lowest monthly payments, and give you the longest repayment options with no prepayment penalty. Next, you'll want to look at the amount of working capital each bank is willing to offer you. Working capital is the amount of money you'll receive after purchasing a practice to cover bills for the first few months. Afterwards, I would suggest seeking a line of credit to be issued after the loan is paid off. A line of credit is money you can withdraw from your account if you need it. Interest is not charged on any line of credit accounts unless you withdraw from it. Most banks provide you a set amount of time to make lower monthly payments prior to expecting you to make a full payment. These are some key areas to consider when evaluating potential loan offers.

I remember I had qualified for a $240,000 loan with a 5.5% interest rate and a 10-year repayment term with Bank of America. Additionally, I made fifteen months of interest-only payments before the full amount was due.

My loan stipulations were:
1. $100,000 for the build-out cost on a 1,235 sq. ft. space
2. $100,000 for furniture, fixtures, equipment and opening order of frames
3. $40,000 working capital
4. Previous debt consolidation into this loan for equipment and supplies I had purchased previously
5. To live within 10 miles of the practice
6. To maintain work outside of the practice during the initial period

The loan amount was more than enough to open the practice at the location I selected. It was a working structure that required a low amount of remodeling. What I did not have enough of was working capital and a line of credit, which is the sticking point on almost every loan and where you should pay the most attention to when comparing loan offers from different sources. I think $60,000 was really the amount needed between working capital and a line of credit to survive my first three years. Make sure you get everything in writing. The best practice is to make sure the required responses are submitted by email, not on the phone so you have proof of any conversations regarding your loans. This is a big deal and will set the stage for what the rest of your warm start period will feel like. I encourage you to take your time and be in a rush for nothing. If something feels rushed, pause and make sure you have done your due diligence to obtain a solid deal. Make the banks compete over you since they need to earn your business.

Question: How much will you need to get started? The short answer: a lot. You'll need to design and remodel your space, turn utilities on, furnish and equip your space, buy supplies, solidify the frame inventory, hire staff and pay bills until the practice can afford to sustain on its own. You'll see how much these expenses can vary from practice to practice. There is no absolute formula or right or wrong way to get through this process, but it is important to have a plan. You will initially write the financial section of your business plan based solely on estimates. As time progresses, make sure to go back and recalculate your bottom line. It would be amazing if your practice was fruitful from the start and able to generate enough profit to cover your living expenses, right? My goal is to get you as close to that scenario as possible. The unfortunate reality for most of us is that it takes time to reach that goal. During that time your working capital and/or line of credit should be enough to operate your business. Outside of that, you'll need to decide how to continue to maintain your cost of living.

The best-case scenario would be already having about six months of living expenses saved up. This way you can devote all your time to running your new practice without the stress of keeping up with home finances too. Therefore, I advise you to build your savings before starting this process. If you have working capital remaining from your business loan, then you might be tempted to use that money to cover other expenses. I would highly recommend keeping that money in the bank and doing some fill-in work outside of your practice. I was moonlighting for about eighteen months after opening my practice.

You can choose to get more equipment upfront and work it into your projected loan and pay less monthly or you can start with a lower loan amount initially and a year or two later buy it and then pay more monthly since it would be 3-5 year payment period so cost more on a monthly basis. No one will have a perfect formula but once you truly have a plan and work the plan you will be fine.

Designing Your Space

When opening a practice, you need to consider the type of atmosphere you intend on creating. A common mistake some optometry business owners make is trying to be everything for everyone. Optometry is known as the "jack-of-all-trades master of none" profession. This phrase can correlate to creating an office environment that is inviting to the clientele you intended on marketing towards. The practice that is considered a high-end optical boutique usually doesn't include Medicaid patients. The ocular disease specialist usually doesn't work in vision therapy. Trying to combine those, especially at the start, can bring you to a place of failure.

If you choose to be a high-end gallery type of practice, then you'd want to carry some funky and unique frames that are not commonly found. If you choose to be a volume practice, purchase an edger to cut your own lenses, find bulk value frames that offer good margins, and get to work. If you choose to do vision therapy, I hope you have a true passion and desire to help children. I suggest making sure your practice has room to spread out and to connect with local pediatricians. These are all very different plans of action, but they can be successful and profitable. You want your space to look like a fully completed thought process that was well put together. Imagine yourself in every corner of your location. Envision what the patient will see, where your staff will be, and how you plan to utilize every square inch of the space.

Obtain Build Out Quotes

If you don't want to go totally grey during the process of building out your space, then slow down when selecting a contractor. This is as important as choosing the right spouse. I suggest you meet with at least three contractors to discuss the scope of the project. Then send out a request for a proposal or RFP. Give contractors a deadline to return a quote. If they cannot meet this deadline, they won't meet any of the other deadlines either. I would then compare all the quotes at the same time and don't necessarily go with the cheapest one but the most thorough and the contractor you feel the best connection with. Never and I repeat NEVER give the contractors all your funds upfront! If you do, then you increase the chances of them NOT completing your project. I suggest paying for the materials directly and making payments on the total cost of labor. You can either specify a price for certain jobs or a percentage of work completed. This part just depends on the amount of work you are willing to do and your comfort level with the scope of the project.

Don't Rush The Process

I remember when time seemed to be moving so fast and everything required a rush decision on my part. Looking back now, slowing down is some of the best advice I would've given my younger self. Visualize yourself in the space, stand in every corner and imagine what the patient would view. Walk through the practice space as an employee and think about what would help with efficiencies. This is the moment when working for other practices really does showcase a benefit for your vision. I hope you've been taking notes along the way because now is the time to compile these notes into a master plan. You'll have this amazing design in your head, see it come to fruition, and realize you must have been drunk when you came up with that color scheme. Be meticulous with the details and a student of the craft.

Branding

There is a huge difference between branding and marketing, and most business owners do not know this. The brand is the essence of the business and marketing is what you do to promote the brand. When I mention the word Ferrari, what is the image you see in your mind? What about Coca-Cola soft drinks? Now I want you to visualize Jordan sneakers. Did you believe that you could finally dunk once you got those shoes? That's what brand recognition is, and consistent marketing efforts reinforce brand dynamics. Think about this - when is the last time you saw a Rolls Royce commercial? When your brand is undeniably recognizable the need for marketing decreases because your business sets the bar to which others hope to reach. You need to decide what the client is going to visualize when they mention the name of your business, come up with a marketing plan, and set it in motion.

What are three components of your brand that you want to create?

_____

_____

_____

_____

Online Presence

Some would say one of the greatest inventions of the 21st century is the Internet, and they are correct. Your online presence is who you are to the world and it is important to establish this in the beginning stages of your business-building goals. You'll want to first research and add your business listing. Starting with a Google listing would be the best way to go as that is the top search site for information on the web. This will require setting up an account and receiving a code from Google in the mail to prove you have access to the location you are claiming. Additionally, you can add photos, videos and as much content that the listing will allow.

Next, I would ask current patients to give you honest reviews about the practice and care you have provided them. You want to encourage reviews and maintain consistent activity on your listings to help you rise in online search rankings. I would then move on to Yelp, Facebook, and Bing just to name a few. Patients are not going to know you personally before they become a patient, so your web presence is who you are to them. After you've completed your setup of free marketing tools, you can move on to more advanced aspects like paid advertising. I personally believe that some doctors do not put time into free online branding resources enough. They would try to skip steps and throw money at problems, such as low patient volume, with no improvement since paid advertising could pull potential patients to their listings. I highly encourage you to learn as much as you can about free marketing tools. It may seem tedious now, but you can save yourself a lot of time and headaches in the long run.

The next step in increasing your online presence is responding to reviews, both good and bad. Google and Yelp allow you to reply to reviews as your business. Also, the rules to the game are in constant fluctuation and you need to check in periodically to see what is to be expected. When you reply to a review, the reviewer and everyone else can see what you wrote. Always keep your responses professional and do not release any HIPAA or other classified information. The rule of thumb when replying is to stay generic especially in public spaces. I know and understand all too well that this is much easier said than done especially when you get a negative review.

No matter how hard you try, not every patient is going to like the care you provide, and it is impossible to not drop the ball occasionally. Patients will never post their faults on why services were not delivered as expected. I stand by Michelle Obama's quote, "When they go low, we go high". A solid response to a negative review is, "I sincerely apologize to you for not receiving the level of care you were expecting. I'd like to know what we can do to make your next visit with us more pleasant. Please contact the practice so that we may be of further assistance to you!" Potential patients reading the reviews regarding your practice will feel confident about your ability to ensure customer satisfaction.

Begin Remodeling

We're on our way and the construction phase has now begun! You've built up a bit of buzz from spending time adding your business listings and social media presence. Your new neighbors and potential clients may be walking by and ask questions. Engage by making them guess the type of business being established and reveal a prize if they guess correctly. Have some fun with the window displays in the meantime too. Coming Soon signs encourage a bit of research (and more interest in your business).

Now you've got to make the money stretch, but you aren't sure of A) where you can save money or B) where you should spend it. I suggest spending money on items that are not easy to change nor alter after opening. Would you know the difference between a $2,000 cabinet and a $400 cabinet from IKEA? Do you need $3,000 computers to start or will $500 tablets work? Do you need $300 commercial grade waiting room chairs or can you go to Home Goods and grab a few for $50? Next year you could upgrade the chairs to refresh the practice. Certain pieces of equipment are timeless and won't change with the new year and in those areas, you want to ensure good quality products. A few things that come to mind are exam room chairs, phoropters, a visual field machine, and an autorefractor. These items don't change from year to year nor go out of style too quickly. Usually, if you can buy most of the equipment from one vendor you can save money over using six different vendors for six pieces of equipment. Some practices use consignment frames, so they only pay for the ones that sell. This strategy saves money upfront, but then you pay $30 for a $20 frame when you could have bought them cheaper.

Depending on your banking situation, the strategies provided can be more advantageous to you. During the remodeling phase, you'll want to make frequent stops at the new practice with early morning and late-night visits. Try and schedule weekly meetings with contractors to make sure everything remains on schedule. I would suggest Monday morning meetings since that gives them a full week to accomplish what is asked. As you continue to follow the project, you might make changes due to the visual difference once key components are installed. You will be asked by the contractor to make changes due to what they find or any limitations from the layout chosen. At this stage, you'd want to consider making the best financial decisions even if they seem to be the hardest. The reward will always be the fact that you are just one step closer to becoming an entrepreneur!

Phones, Internet And Alarm System

What do you normally do when the Internet goes down? Or when a credit card machine doesn't work? Or when you can't print anything from a single desktop computer?! These problems will arise, but you must have protocols in place and properly trained staff who know how to handle them. Make sure at least one computer is hard-wired to a printer so even if your practice Wi-Fi goes down you can still maintain printing capabilities. Have a backup payment processor, such as a Square, PayPal, or Stripe card reader, on hand in case your credit card machine malfunctions.

You should also consider having two internet lines or at least a hotspot so when you lose service your business can continue. The alarm and camera systems should have a backup battery so in the event of a storm or crisis the practice is still protected. Most surge protectors can be purchased with a one to two-hour battery back-up. Flexibility regarding your phone, internet, alarms, and camera systems is a must in my opinion. Voice over IP, or VoIP, is an online-based phone system through the internet that can allow you to have numerous phone lines at an affordable price. I, personally, wouldn't go too cheap on phone and internet service. I would, however, get the highest bandwidth I could afford since you'd be working with a lot of data and information both online and offline.

It is a violation of HIPAA rules to have cameras in exam rooms and even some waiting rooms. But placing them in hallways and near the front desk is a wise decision to protect yourself and your staff. Obtaining a HIPAA compliant fax system is very important! Sfax is one of the few HIPAA compliant systems on the market, but other options may become available at later dates. Visible alarms won't deter criminals considering a theft takes seconds not minutes. However, being able to access the alarm system remotely is a beneficial feature to consider. If the alarm is tripped, you can check camera feeds, alert police or fire rescue or notify your staff that you have things under control.

When everything begins to fail, do you have a contingency and/or safety plan?

___ Yes, I am tech-savvy!
___ No, can you repeat what I need to do again?

Insurance Credentialing

Insurance – to accept or not to accept that is the question. The response to this depends on the type of office you are trying to create. Some people will tell you not to take any vision plans and only take medical plans plus attract cash-paying patients. Others would say take every plan that will let you on to get a butt in the chair after you first launch. Every plan and location will have different reimbursements requirements, so you'll need to look at what you'll receive in your area for a particular plan. The benefit of an insurance panel is that you will be listed as an in-network provider for patients, which would encourage them to use their benefits at your location. Some plans are better than others and each one needs to be examined based on what works best for your office. I would judge plans based on these four characteristics:

1. Do they allow you to use your own lab?
2. Do they allow you to earn a profit from contact lens sales?

3. Do they require you to sell their frames?
4. What type of patients do they bring to your office?

Do not be so quick to accept the rate that is first offered by the insurance companies you want to be credentialed with. Compare the numbers and ask yourself if that price point will be fair or will you lose money seeing that patient. Calculate your chair cost. A chair cost is a fixed cost divided by the number of complete exams over a certain time period. This gives you the cost to see a patient even if they buy nothing in your office. Here's an example. If you generally see two patients per hour but need to see three to meet your average chair cost, then that is not a plan you should sign up for. Some parts of a plan can't be adjusted, but others are up for negotiation if you ask. You would be surprised at how many people sign paperwork without reading it. Once you are approved, it will be more difficult to get the insurance company to adjust its terms. Do your research to find out how many opticians in your region accept this plan, how many optical providers the insurance has, and how your office compares to those. If you can show value and the reason why the insurance company should want you as a provider in their network, then you can usually get better terms.

Do not get too frustrated with the process and try to get creative on ways to complete it. Some plans may require you to accept others to get on theirs. Medicare and Medicaid will be some of the most challenging to complete. Hopefully, you were credentialed by some of these plans at your prior place of employment, and when completing applications, you would be adding a new location and not starting from scratch. This process can take 3-6 months to complete and only a few will let you back bill the policy. Back billing means some will allow you to see patients while you are going through paperwork and then bill the plan when the process is over. Be careful doing this since you are not a credentialed provider and benefits have not been officially used so a patient could go across the street after you see them and use that benefit, so that by the time you are on the plan, you don't get paid for that visit. In the beginning, you may want to seek the help of a credentialing company to speed up the process.

There are numerous companies on the market but anything to avoid some headaches in this process will be worth it especially if you get paid faster. As soon as you have keys to the store it's never too early to start the process. You will need a Medicare number before you can do VSP and you will need to be on a few vision plans before you can bill medical in some areas. I would start them all and then work through the issues as they arise. Most applications will ask for similar information so spend the day to write them all out since it will be repetitive. You will need a W-9, NPI, EIN, and CAQH number as a start.

Now Hiring!

You have reached the point where your build-out has finally been completed, furnishings and equipment have been bought, systems are in place and you need to hire staff. Your practice staff will be your greatest asset and greatest challenge. You simply cannot operate a store/practice by yourself, so you'll need at least one other person to bring on board. Who do you hire and for what positions? A general rule of thumb is an optician can be a technician, but not all technicians can sell in optical.

There are numerous places to find good applicants, but the best is through word of mouth referrals. Ask the reps that sell your product if they know of anyone looking for work or are unhappy in their current location. You have a variety of job placement sites to choose from such as Craigslist, Indeed, Monster, and Zip Recruiter. The interview process is more of an art than a science, and no matter how hard you try, you will have a rough time. I ask potential candidates to do a working interview for a day so they can get a feel for how I operate, and I can see if they are a good fit for our practice culture.

There will be times when a person has a solid interview, but then turns out to not be the best fit for the position they are applying for. It doesn't mean that they were bad at their job, but usually, they were in the wrong position in the practice. Some would suggest giving a DISC profile test to potential staffers to evaluate the personality characteristics they would bring into the practice. Sometimes you must figure out if you have the wrong people on the bus or if you have the right people on the bus but in the wrong position, which doesn't allow them to excel.

I would suggest hiring slow and firing fast. Try to refrain from hiring employees to do the jobs you don't want to do. View them as an extension of yourself. You should know how to do everything in the office. New hires would require some level of training and guidance. Now a good employee would eventually be better than you in a specific area or two, but there will come a day when you'll need to dispense glasses or lookup insurance. Learn while it is slow and that will pay off for you later.

Choosing An EHR System

I suggest starting with an electronic health records (EHR) system right from the beginning. The EHR is the lifeblood of your practice and taking the time to understand how it works can maximize and greatly benefit your practice. How you manage going forward will depend on if you integrate with your EHR. Find a well-known company that has good customer service and positive reviews. Take your time with this step and once you make your decision, go for it. The headache of trying to switch from paper charts after you've gained clientele and have become much busier is not what you want.

There are several EHR programs on the market and each one will differ on what it provides. The first question you'll need to ask yourself is do you want it to be cloud-based or server-based? The on-site server system would be faster and not dependent on your Internet speed, but it may be more cumbersome to access records outside the practice. With a server-based system, you may require the help of an IT professional to make sure documents are being saved and routed correctly. Most of the cost in a server-based system can be front-loaded into your loan and lower your monthly bills.

The benefit of a cloud-based EHR system is that you can access it anywhere within the practice, but that depends on your wireless setup. Cloud-based EHR has a lower upfront cost and a higher monthly payment, plus you risk a rising cost as you increase the amount of staff you hire. If you don't have a lot of money left on your loan, then this might be a good option. Remember you will have a bill that adds up over time. There is no such thing as a perfect system, but you can find one that works best for your business.

What are some key factors that are most important to you in an EHR system?

_____

_____

Frame Inventory

This part of the process requires you to be very methodical. The rule here is you can always buy more products, but you can't get that money back. Until you start seeing a steady flow of patients, it will be difficult to know what clients want in your area. Try not to buy a product that overlaps or covers the same category of patients.

According to industry trends, most practices have 60 to 40 percent women to men as patients and you want that reflected in your optical offerings. Women go to the doctor more it's a proven fact. If you plan to offer services for myopia control, then you'll need to have a good collection of kids' frames. If your practice will be more of a boutique, then you will want to consider unique frames from Buffalo Horn and Wood. And if you're going fully fashion-forward, then offer Bespoke or 3D generated glasses. Hands down the best place to shop for eyewear would be at Vision Expo that happens twice a year in Las Vegas and New York City. I suggest attending the show prior to making any selections so you can see the frames, compare quality and negotiate the best deals.

The frames you offer define the soul and essence of your optical store. Do you want brands that patients can find at any store in your area or do you want to have your own private label where the frames you offer are yours and leave out other companies? Going the private label route allows a patient to promote your brand through admiration of the style of frames they're wearing. What is the demographic of the neighborhood and what type of patients are you trying to attract? You want to make sure you have frames that allow you to be profitable at any price point. It is up to you to navigate the patients' needs and wants or let the patients drive you on the type of optical business you will have.

What insurances will your practice accept? I encourage you to exercise caution when purchasing frames under the wholesale frame allowance (WFA) specified by the insurance companies with which you participate. If the frame is under a WFA, then you will only be reimbursed for the wholesale cost and you can't charge the patient anything additional. Here's an example. Let's say the highest WFA for a plan is $65. You order frames at $70 then mark them up to $240. A patient has an allowance of $150 with a 20 percent discount on the overage. You charge the patient $72 plus you get the WFA back from the insurance company. If you were to sell that same patient a frame that wholesaled at $60 you would only receive that amount back. In another example, let's say the patient wanted covered frames. You would want to have frames with a wholesale cost of $65, but you receive a 20-30 percent discount. You would make some money back on those frames plus you could sell the patient lenses for an additional price to offset the loss. You have so many options to choose from. My suggestion? Purchase with your business goals in mind. Every decision you make should match up to the vision and mission statements you wrote previously.

Equip Your Office

Let's get the core parts of your practice in place. This process will require keeping track of your budget and spreadsheet to make sure everything is ordered. Even with the best planning, you might forget to order something, or you'll order the wrong product. Relax, it happens to the best of us. Grab a pen and pad and go through the practice with these two questions:

1. To complete an eye exam what will we need?
2. To order glasses what will we need?

My rule of thumb is if the technology won't change very much in five years, then I am willing to spend the necessary amount. This should include chairs, stands, slit lamp, phoropter, visual field, autorefractor, and fundus camera. If you follow this rule there are still some exceptions. Will the cost to get the latest and greatest be worth it? That depends considering a patient won't notice the difference between the $4,000 option and the $14,000 one. I would suggest getting a digital phoropter or manual. Some patients may mention how fancy your practice is during the exam, but some things never really go out of style. It's still the thought of which is better in this room. I will agree that once you pass 10 full exams a day your shoulder will be happy you splurged on the digital phoropter. Only you know your budget.

I would suggest looking at manufacturers such as Zeiss, Marco, or Lombart for the digital phoropter. Each company will have its own way of showcasing the digital phoropter format. Go to a local trade show and check them out or ask a local rep to bring one to your practice and allow you to test drive it for a few days. This is the bread and butter of your profession so get something you like. The next items that are an area of contention would be a standard fundus camera versus ultra-widefield photography. This is an area of emerging technology that is getting lots of attention.

In more affluent areas, patients may be used to paying extra for wide-field photography. Now imaging is not a substitute for dilation, but some patients won't come back for dilation appointments no matter how much you try to convince them. Having a picture of the peripheral retina when assessing each patient is a pretty big ordeal. Looking into the back of the eye is like looking into outer space. Make sure you have a large monitor to review images with each patient and get ready for the positive reviews. Ultra-wide field photography is a real wow factor and can really increase word of mouth referrals from current patients. For these pieces of equipment, investigate Zeiss, Optos or Centervue.

Next up is deciding on a lab to use for your lenses. This decision will come from the connections you make with lab reps in the area. As a new practice, they may have some promotions to help you get started since your volume will be low. Some of the buying groups you join may have already worked out deals with labs to help you save on the cost of goods. As your volume grows you may venture out and find new labs that will give you great deals and service to win over your business.

One big-time saving I received when I first opened was a frame tracer. The tracer would allow you to trace the shape of the frame and digitally transmit that to the lab so they could begin working on lenses immediately instead of waiting two to three days for frames to arrive. This increased the turnaround time to get the product back and improve the overall customer experience. I would suggest narrowing down the list of options you allow your opticians to choose from so that you maintain control of the product that leaves your store. Now, remember when I said to wait to purchase the edger? Well, this is where waiting could benefit you in the long run. Depending on the lab you sign up with you may be able to get the lab to split the cost of the edger if you agree to send a certain number of requests to that lab.

Every area of the country will have certain labs that are more popular, but I would compare Zeiss, Essior, Hoya, and Shamir labs and see who'll offer the best bang for your buck. It's easier to compare companies when you have narrowed down your product offerings. I would heed caution against solely focusing on the price points since one lab can promise you a dollar cheaper but take a week longer to deliver the product. Some labs offer customer support and back-end support to help educate staff with lifelong learning. Building two-way relationships in this business will continue to benefit you in the long run.

Next, let's look at major contact lens brands. I would suggest picking the two companies that have had the most successful fittings with your patients and order with them initially. Now, choosing the suppliers might be the difficult part. You will not be busy enough to be on anyone's radar initially but clumping all your sales in a few bundles will help build relationships with a few of these suppliers. When you start, some companies will provide you with an inside sales rep instead of a local rep in the area. You may also have a difficult time receiving the initial contact lens fitting sets since they are very expensive to produce, and small practices will have low volume initially. This is what separates a rep from a consultant. The consultant can see that by supporting your small practice you can grow together. This was one of the ways I chose who I supported since they supported me. You will lean on the representative from that company more as a consultant in that industry and the advice they give to you and your staff can really make a huge impact on your bottom line. Hopefully, you have already been working in the area for a while so you may already have a working relationship with these companies. If not, contact Bausch and Lomb, Cooper Vision, Alcon, and/or J&J Vision to get started. You will also have the option to order the product directly with each company or through a distributor.

Most doctors will use a distributor but once again look to the buying group for a narrowed list with the best terms possible. The benefit of using a distributor usually means faster delivery of any product they have in stock. When you use a distributor, you can clump together your orders from different companies for the day into one order to reduce your shipping cost. I would pay attention to the price you are supposed to pay for an item and make sure the distributor is giving you the agreed-upon number. This is an area that can be worked on as you get settled.

Office Supplies

After purchasing all the high dollar equipment, there are still dozens of other items needed. They may be smaller in cost, but that cost can add up if you're not careful. After you receive all your frames you will need a place to display them. This is one area you can save on initially and add in fancier options later. There are a ton of frame board manufacturers that can sell you displays, but I encourage you to think outside the box! Look online for bookshelves and glass cabinets. Get creative and retrofit old furniture.

The more unique and out-of-the-box the display is, the better the impression it will leave on your patients. Home Depot and a can of spray paint can be your best friend. Amazon and IKEA have great selections and all you may need is a screwdriver, some friends and a few boxes of pizza.

You will still need a bunch of smaller items such as birthday postcards, appointment reminder cards, stamps, envelopes, pens, markers, printing paper, etc. At my practice, I laminated the entrance forms and then use dry erase markers to have patients fill out forms to save on paper. For the restroom, I bought two hundred white hand towels and washed those weekly to save on paper towel usage. You will need enough computers for your staff, a laser printer, a color printer and a scanner. You'll also need dilating drops, dilation glasses, and cotton tip applicators. This reminds me of a joke from the movie "Coming to America" that was added after the credits finished rolling. One of Eddie Murphy's characters was asking the waiter to taste the soup he just put in front of him. The waiter asks if the soup was too hot or cold. Eddie tells the person to just taste the soup. The waiter asks him where the spoon is. Always remember to put yourself in the shoes of others and see if you see things more clearly.

ENDGAME
Checkmate

"Resistance is the greatest just before the finish line."
– Steven Pressfield

Policies And Procedures Manual

It is important for you to create a policies and procedures manual. This document will outline how each process in your business should be carried out. An effective manual is a difference between a practice that's dependent on the owner to function or a business that can operate without the owner being present. It will be a daunting task to break down every duty and describe exactly how it should be done but starting now can save you time in the future. I've included a list of questions under the top three topics below to help you get started. These questions below pertain to your opening procedures:

- What will your practice/store hours be?
- Who is responsible for opening the practice/store? What time are they expected to arrive/clock-in?
- Is there an alarm to be disarmed? If so, who knows the code?

- Are there certain duties that should be completed before the practice opens for the day's business, i.e. an opening checklist to follow?
- What is the earliest and latest time a patient can be seen?
- What should the practice look like, sound and smell like when they enter the doors?
- Who should greet the patients and how?

The check-in process is usually the first face-to-face interaction your patients have with your staff. Perfecting this encounter is mandatory. It's at this point where the business begins to earn the trust and respect of its patients.

These next questions pertain to your check-in procedures:

- Is there paperwork to fill out physically or has it already been done online?
- Has the patients' insurance already been verified? If so, when?

- How much time will be allotted for the check-in process?
- Which staff position is responsible for each part of the check-in process?
- Are any payments collected at check-in?
- What do the patients do while waiting for their appointment?
- Is there a specific place where they wait?
- What is the policy on late arrivals?

Pre-testing is usually the next step of the process. It is very common for pre-testing to vary for different patients and exams. Having these differences clearly written out and easy to reference will ensure that you have all the information you need at exam time whether it's your full-time technician administering the tests or a fill-in optician.

These next questions pertain to your pre-testing processes:
- How is the patient-directed from the reception area into the clinic area?

- When a technician is interacting with the patient during pre-testing, what types of questions do you want to be answered?
- What do they do for a living that is visually demanding?
- What do they do for fun that is visually demanding?
- How did they hear about the practice?
- How do you want the patient room set up when you enter?

Take some time to really ponder on your ideal standard of operations. Don't get too caught up on providing the best answers. By the end of this exercise, you will have a solid starter document.

Train Employees

After finding the perfect first employee, you will need to train them. There is no shortage of programs and training modules offered usually at little to no cost. First, contact your lab and see if they have any programs for training. Then look at your chosen buying group and, most of the time, they have training courses available for you. After you have exhausted your resources the best trainer you have is you. Only you know exactly how you want office tasks to be completed. In the beginning, it should be slow enough for you to have time to get your hands in there and accomplish each task yourself along with your trainee.

Staff will continuously be the hardest part of this endeavor you are about to embark on. The rule that was told to me and still holds true today - hire slow, fire fast. Once you have staff on board keeping them going in the right direction can present a challenge. I suggest holding morning meetings to go over expectations and what needs to be done for that day before it starts. Then hold monthly staff meetings to review the previous month and highlight the good along with areas that need improvement. School can teach you how to do an eye exam, but they don't teach you how to manage people effectively.

Employee training must be a consistent practice in your office. The same way you would learn every day your staff will do the same. This is where a policy and procedure manual will come in handy. You should have written out exactly how you want various office work done and specific job descriptions for each employee. You cannot hold someone accountable if they do not know what they are being held accountable for. The clearer and more concise you are in the beginning the fewer headaches you will have in the end.

Marketing Campaign

It is time to work on your marketing campaign. If you have the money available, you can pay a marketing specialist or consultant to create and implement marketing strategies for your business. If you don't have the extra funds, then you will have to use your own time to work on your campaigns or hire a technician who has a marketing background. Your goal with any marketing plan is to increase your customer volume and sales.

When a consumer sees your ad, they may place you in two categories – to fulfill an immediate need or to come to you for future use. Remember, other companies may have a larger marketing budget to work with. They may have more convenient hours of operation or accept all vision insurance. What exactly makes your business more unique than the others in your area? Would you choose you when looking at options knowing nothing about the practice personally? These are questions to think about as you work towards your marketing strategies.

Before you spend any money or time in marketing you need to learn about your consumer and what is called a "customer avatar" or consumer profile. You'll need to know how and where they spend money, how and where they absorb content, where they live, their ages, lifestyles and more to make sure your money and effort reach its maximum effectiveness. If one of your goals were to attract older consumers, then print ads and mailers, while more expensive, could yield a higher return on your investment over social media ads.

If one of your goals were to attract the younger trendier consumers, then social media ads, with the potential to cost you less, are the way to go. One key thing about social media is that it requires you to be social - somewhat. If you are a private person and don't desire to use social media, then I suggest having one of your staff members create and monitor social media business accounts.

Social media has numerous platforms, and each requires a different marketing strategy. Instagram, for example, is all about using pictures and short videos to provide a glimpse into one's life. You can now use longer videos on IGTV and share stories with your followers and consumers. For Facebook, you'll need a picture and/or video ad to reach consumers. With Facebook and Instagram, you can narrow your audience down to the soccer mom who likes wheatgrass juice, kale salads, and plays tennis as part of your consumer profile. But this requires a steady stream of content, a marketing plan, and strategies to execute. LinkedIn is an online business-to-business platform. It is rare that you would gain a customer from this site, but you can stay connected to industry insiders and professionals like me!

The tried and true method of using print ads is not dead! Look into an Every Door Direct Mailer, or EDDM, provider in your area or online. They will deliver a postcard to everyone on the mail carriers' route at a reduced price and you don't have to individually address each house. For this strategy to be effective, you'll need to create a sense of urgency within the advertisement. Maybe you'd offer a discount on a service if they bring the card to their initial exam within 30 days. Maybe they get a free glasses cleaning kit just for stopping in with the ad. It can work if you work it! It is suggested that you an area with one thousand houses and send mailers to the area about three times instead of sending mailers to three thousand houses at once. Most people need repeated reinforcement before they act so if at first you don't succeed try, try again!

Email marketing, to your existing patients, could be considered the cheapest and most effective way to market, yet most practices underutilize this tool. These people have already come and experienced your amazing practice and you want to encourage them to refer their family and friends to receive that same great service? Email marketing is the way to go. You can inform them of any openings you have available on your schedule during school or bank holidays. Just a reminder that they can utilize your services on a day they have off is sometimes enough to fill up a schedule. You can also advertise specials on lenses and frames or offer exclusive discounts if they show you the ad in the email or provide a coupon code.

Before I go any further, I want to bring up this important rule - don't pass out cards, build relationships. The BEST form of marketing, in my opinion, is to get out in the community and meet people. I can easily forget the person who just shoved their card in my face or hand, but I'll generally remember the person I sat and ate a snack with and talked to about current events. Relationships last a lifetime. Cards last until I get home, empty my pockets, and throw it away.

Open House

"Go Big or Go Home!" It's time to make a splash! Invite everyone you've ever met or connected within your life. You could even host multiple open houses. You've got family and friends first, then a thank you to all the reps and construction crew, and lastly fully open to the public and everyone in the neighborhood. A challenge you'll face is to find the customer and get them to walk through your doors.

Open houses are not just for fun seeing as you are on the clock. Your goal is to sell glasses, contacts and make appointments for future exams. You have a captive audience that loves and supports you at that moment. If they can drive to your practice for a party, then they can drive for an exam. You want to capture names, addresses, phone numbers and email addresses of everyone that attends. If you don't take a picture of the event, then it never happened. Hire a photographer to take pictures and videos to share with attendees and future customers. If someone notices themselves in the content captured, then the likelihood of them sharing it increases exponentially. Let me burst your bubble now – this may not go according to plan and you could make mistakes. The thought process to combat this is that your practice is a play and the clients are the audience who have never seen this play. Therefore, so the show must go on!

Most people will bypass the mistakes made after you first open. All you need to do is to breathe and keep performing. Once the buzz from your open house wears off and you have seen all your friends and family as patients you must do ensure you concentrate your efforts on marketing to remind people that you're open. After I opened, I didn't do trunk shows like some of my colleagues since most of my patients would have come to the practice and seen the inventory. Instead, I found other reasons for patients to walk through our doors. Network with local authors and have book release events. Think outside the box and have a fashion show in the practice by teaming up with local clothing stores. The models could wear colored contacts or a funky frame that will be available from your practice. How about connecting with local artists by hosting a live painting session or spoken word events? Fundraisers for local charities in the practice are a big hit as well.

Open For Business!

Opening day is a special day. It's something you will remember forever. If possible, plan for your first set of patients. Perform some exams on staff so that they can help you work out the kinks and there will always be kinks. When an issue comes up, take a deep breath and find a solution.

You have read this book and took meticulous notes, so now what? Starting a business will teach you patience. You must be present to win. Whenever you are in the office there is always something to do, whether it be to create an educational post for social media, updating your practice manual, or sending out handwritten thank you cards, there should never be a wasted moment.

The one thing that I believe freaks out most optometrists is not the opening, but it is if they can handle the administrative work that it takes to run a business. The short answer to that question is YES! Your major concerns will be rent, payroll, utilities, and cost of goods sold (COG). Of course, there will be small bills here and there, but you won't lose sleep over that. A forty-dollar water bill should not keep you up at night. You will survive another month. This is where having that line of credit and six months of expenses saved will give you the calm to weather the storm. That is the part that stops lots of docs from making the leap into private practice and for those that read to the end you should be ready to go.

At the end of the day it takes time to build a great practice and you cannot rush the process. If you can look at yourself in the mirror and say I did the best I could today, then you have done enough. Just be patient.

I know that you know that you aren't perfect. Your practice isn't going to be perfect and your patients aren't going to be perfect. Every day is a new day and another opportunity to be amazing.

We get into private practice for different reasons, but we want to control our own destiny and enjoy life the way we see fit. Although in the beginning, you may need to work eighty hours for yourself to avoid working forty hours for someone else. You will need to take breaks to recharge your batteries. Recognize when you have reached your limit and need to rest and revitalize. Drink lots of water, eat more fruits and vegetables, and exercise to maintain a healthy balance. Become a tourist in your own neighborhood. Go out and meet your neighbors, support their businesses and make friends. It is good for your health, for your soul and for your future practice!

The Master Checklist

___ Do you know your WHY?
___ Wrote description of your perfect office
___ Selected the name of your business
___ Wrote your Mission Statement
___ Wrote your Vision Statement
___ Saved 6 months of personal fixed expenses
___ Have you secured your social media handles?
___ Have you pulled your credit report?
___ What are the top 3 cities you would like your office located in?
___ Can you survive on 3 days a week of your salary?
___ NPI number created?
___ CAQH number received?
___ EIN secured
___ Trademark Submitted
___ Checking account opened
___ Decided on a consultant
___ Selected a buying group
___ Selected a space to open your business
___ Secured financing
___ Selected a contractor
___ What is your Brand narrative?
___ Started insurance credentialing
___ Began hiring process
___ Selected an EHR system
___ Decided on a curated collection of frames
___ Order miscellaneous supplies and items
___ Created an office manual
___ Decided on Marketing Strategy
___ Planned Open house

___ Sent this book to a friend
___ Post about this book using #OptometryChess hashtag

Appendix

Accounting
https://www.adp.com
https://qbo.intuit.com
https://www.mint.com

Billing
https://www.apexedi.com
https://www.availity.com
https://www.backintheblacksolutions.com
http://www.claimdoctor.net
http://gatewayedi.com
https://optometricbilling.com

Buying Groups
https://idoc.net
https://www.healthyeyesadvantage.com
https://www.pecaa.com
http://www.percalliance.com
https://visionsource.com
https://www.vtrends.us

Contact Lens Distributors
https://www.abboptical.com/
https://www.e-dr.com
https://oogp.com
https://wisvis.com

Conferences
https://www.aaopt.org
https://nationaloptometricassociation.com
http://www.optometrysmeeting.org

https://secointernational.com
www.VisionExpo.com
www.BlackEyecarePerspective.com

Consulting Companies
https://www.cleinman.com
https://icareadvisors.com
https://www.powerpractice.com
https://the.vg
https://www.thewilliamsway.com
www.BlackEyecarePerspective.com
https://www.corcoranccg.com

Contact Lens
https://www.bausch.com
https://www.myalcon.com
https://coopervision.com
https://www.jnjvisionpro.com

Data Analytics
https://edge30.gatewaypn.com
https://www.glimpselive.com

Electronic Health Records
http://crystalpm.com
http://foxfiresg.com
https://itrust.io
https://www.revolutionehr.com

Frame Companies
http://www.luxottica.com/en
https://marchon.com
http://www.safilogroup.com/en/

Getting Started Resources
https://nppes.cms.hhs.gov/#/
https://proview.caqh.org/
https://www.irs.gov/businesses/small-businesses-self-employed/apply-for-an-employer-identification-number-ein-online
https://www.cms.gov/Medicare/Provider-Enrollment-and-Certification/MedicareProviderSupEnroll/index.html

Lens Manufacturers
https://www.essilorusa.com
https://www.hoyavision.com
https://www.shamirlens.com
https://www.zeiss.com

Miscellaneous
https://www.papermart.com
http://www.storminnormans.com
https://www.continualcompliance.com/
http://www.odspecs.com

Medical Coding
https://decisionmakerplus.net
http://eyecor.com
https://www.codesafeplus.com
http://www.eyecodingforum.com/main/
https://www.medicaloptometriccare.com

Other Resources
E-Myth Optometrist by Michael E. Gerber
A Different Perspective by Alan H. Cleinman

201 Secrets of a High Performance Optometric Practice by Bob Levoy
How to Measure and Improve Team Productivity in a Private Practice Optometry by Jerry Hayes
Practice Management in Optometry by Gailmard OD, Neil

Phone And Marketing Companies
https://www.demandforce.com
https://eyecareprime.com
https://www.solutionreach.com
https://www.weavehelp.com/

* I have no financial affiliation with any of the companies listed

Made in United States
Orlando, FL
26 July 2023